# A Brief Guide To The Modern Job Market

# By

# T.A. DeLozier

# 1. ABOUT THIS BOOK

"I need a new job, now!" I get it. Trust me, I hear you loud and clear. I have been in your shoes and I am going to tell you what works and the mindset you need to have to get a job in today's market. Today's job market might as well be the wild west. There are no clearly defined rules and human resources professionals can't agree on a one-size-fits-all answer for you getting a job. They are looking for the best candidates to fill the open jobs they have. It could be you, but they probably won't ever see your resume. That doesn't mean you should give up, that means you must learn the rules of engagement and learn to play by their rules. Many large companies have a strict hiring process, and for them to violate their sacred hiring processes is considered nothing short of blasphemy.

In this book, I am going to tell what your strategy needs to be, regardless of your level of education. I don't assume that you are a Harvard business school graduate, like most job hunting books do. No, I will assume that you are a human being, looking for a paycheck, a way to effectively make ends meet. However, just in case you are interested in the education debate, I have made a chapter for that topic as well. So, grab a cup of coffee and let me teach you a few things about the job market.

When I was a younger adult, the United States Air Force taught me a valuable lesson. No one cares about your lack of self-confidence, your ego, or your pride. None of those things have any kind of logical argument in your life. I give you permission to throw those things away and learn things that you had no idea are possible. Do not ever think that you can't get a better job, and don't try to argue with me in your mind either. I'm going to do what I can to help you. In this book, I side with the job seeker. I am here for you.

> *"Learn the rules of the game. And then you can play better than anyone else."* -Albert Einstein

# 2. SHOULD I GET A COLLEGE DEGREE?

I could write an entire book on the education debate. I call it a debate because there are many views on whether a college degree is truly necessary. While it is true that there are a lot of elitist companies out there who require even their lowest level employees to have master's degrees from the most prestigious schools on the planet, there are still a lot of companies who don't really focus on your education, they want to know your accomplishments, your experience, and the kinds of skills that you possess. Some of the sharpest people I have ever met and even worked for were high ranking individuals who don't have more than a high school diploma. So, should you get a college education? I would say that you should if you want to. It could boost your chances of getting a better job, but there is also no guarantee. Also, don't go into debt if you are going to get an "easy degree" that won't give you the skills you need to succeed in the modern job market. You also don't need to go to college to learn the skills that they teach. You can very easily download a course catalogue from a well-known university and buy your own books for each subject and teach yourself. Save your money!

Let's look more closely at getting a degree and other learning opportunities that are available.

## 2.1. GOING BACK TO SCHOOL

If you want to go back to school, you absolutely should. Just keep in mind you don't have to. There are some things that you should know. I went to school and loved it so much that after earning a bachelor's degree in business administration (BSBA), I continued and earned a master's degree in business administration (MBA). My education made me aware of how little I really knew as an individual and that my education doesn't ever stop, even after earning my degrees.

Before you decide to go back to school, ask yourself if you even have time to do so. Finding an online school might be the best option. If this is something that you are interested in, make sure that the online institution is accredited. Accreditation is easy to determine, all you have to do is go to the United States Department of Education website. The website also has all kinds of relevant information on going back to school. This website will be essential in deciding the best institution to attend, based on your needs. Going back to school is a serious commitment. If you are serious about going back to school, start looking at potential institutions and see if you can speak with an admissions advisor. An admissions advisor can go over the application and enrollment processes with you.

### 2.1.1. AVERAGE LEVEL OF INCOME BY EDUCATION

It should be no secret to anyone that a college education has the potential of increasing one's earnings considerably; however, this is not guaranteed. I have created a chart below, that provides a detailed overview of how your earnings may dramatically increase after gaining a 2-year education and beyond. Keep in mind that these numbers are simply averages of each sample of the United States population, as a result, you might be making more or less than what is being stated here. As well, there are thousands of jobs that require a degree. The Bureau of Labor statistics website provides a lot of helpful career field information.

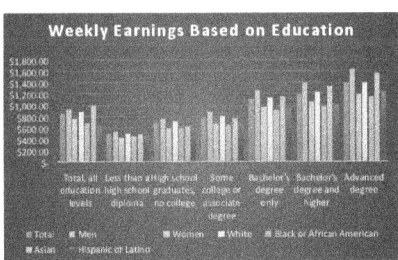

(Bureau of Labor Statistics, 2015)

### 2.2. NOT GOING BACK TO SCHOOL

Just as going to school has its advantages, not going to school also has its advantages as well. For one, you don't have to pay back any student loans. I came to the realization during my graduate course work, that I could have downloaded a free course catalogue and read various books on each subject myself, instead of shelling out almost $1,000.00 per class. When was the last time you visited a local book store, or even browsed around the Amazon Kindle shop on your smart phone? You really don't have to go into debt to learn valuable skills. I have worked for several skilled managers who never attended college and they have all used a similar method. The resources that are available to you may still cost you money, but they are more affordable and would allow you to focus on skills that are strictly relevant to your career goals.

### 2.2.1. LINKEDIN LEARNING

I didn't find out about LinkedIn learning until after I was already in school and actively looking for a decent job. When you subscribe to LinkedIn premium you not only get premium job searching statistics, you also have access to thousands of computer-based training courses, that teach a wide variety of professional skills. When you complete a course, you earn a certificate to prove your knowledge. This is probably one of the best college alternatives in my opinion. I recommend this option to people who prefer information presented to them and have a visual learning style. LinkedIn learning also has printouts that give you application-based projects to work on, depending on the course. LinkedIn offers everyone a free trial month. Think about a skill that you want to learn and try it for yourself. A LinkedIn subscription is much more affordable than going back to school.

### 2.2.2. "BUY THE BOOK" APPROACH

If you are a book person like me, just buy a book about a skill that you are interested in. If you are extremely passionate about a skill, buy multiple books on it. You don't have to be guided by a distinguished professor. We have books so that everyone can learn something. Books are secret treasures hidden in plain sight. Be someone who takes advantage of them. I have lost track of how many books that I have purchased over the years for the various subjects that I have been interested in.

When it comes to books, you can either purchase physical copies, or you can purchase digital versions. The digital copies may be the most convenient, especially on Google books. Google allows you to highlight portions of the text and assign your own notes as you read. This makes it easy to find information that you need to reference for later. Amazon Kindle has the same feature. I have found this feature useful when conducting my own studies.

### 2.3. THOUGHTS ON THE COLLEGE DEBATE

T.A. DeLozier

How the culture views a college education is paradoxical in nature, whereas many of those that do not have one feel that the only way to get a decent job is to have a college degree. Many of those that have a college degree often find out that a college education only serves as a mere bullet point on their resume. So, what is the final answer to the college degree question? Only you can hope to answer that. What does a college education mean to you? Are you after a degree, or are you after the education? If you look at a degree as a golden ticket to make more money, nothing could be further from the truth. You would be one of millions who used federal funds to earn a degree that means absolutely nothing to an employer. Now, if you are seeking an education, a chance to learn valuable skills, college would be a good place for you. Keep in mind, where you go to school does not matter, as long as the school is accredited. There are employers that will only hire from accredited colleges if a degree is required for the position. An accredited education is considered a legitimate one. If you need to use federal funds, you need to familiarize yourself with the industry that you are interested in and see if the education will be able to pay for itself. This is how you can increase your chances of seeing returns from this long-term investment. The more you know, the more tools you will have in your arsenal. This has the potential of increasing your value in your chosen field. Some skills can even be carried over into multiple fields.

## 2.4. CHAPTER CONCLUSION

Remember, each choice has its benefits and concerns, you just have to decide which option or combination of options that is right for you. If you go back to school and take out student loans, try to pick a field that will be able to pay for itself. If you are looking to improve one or two skills, check out LinkedIn learning; you will save yourself a lot of money. I didn't want to go into too much depth in this chapter about the college debate, there are countless resources out there that can argue for and against each point. Each side has a compelling argument, but I feel each person must decide for themselves, what direction they should take in their own career.

# 3. WHAT ABOUT MY RESUME?

Your resume may be the first thing that an employer sees when considering you for potential employment. This will be the most critical aspect of your job hunt. If your resume is not appropriately formatted and leaves out key words, relevant to the position you are applying for, it is likely that no one will ever see your resume. Your resume should have the following points:

|         |                                                          |                                                                                                                                                                            |
| ------- | -------------------------------------------------------- | -------------------------------------------------------------------------------------------------------------------------------------------------------------------------- |
| **Point 1** | Neatly format your name and contact information | You need to provide your name and contact information, so each potential employer can easily contact you if they would like to schedule a phone screening. |
| **Point 2** | List your academic degrees and any certifications you have. | You will want to list all your academic skills first because these |

|  |  | are going to give any potential employer a brief overview of your formal education (if applicable). |
|---|---|---|
| **Point 3** | List only your relevant job experience. | Try to list only your last 3 positions. Only list accomplishments that are relevant to the job that you are applying for. This point is the most important. Most recruiters only search for relevant key words in their applicant tracking systems. |

With each point, be as brief as possible. Do your absolute best to showcase your proudest achievements. This was never meant to be a complicated process. However, there are still countless resources that provide more detail on how to create the best resume. You can even purchase software that can write your resume for you into the desired format. Remember, this is your career. Do whatever you can to make your resume the best it can be.

Once you have finished your resume, proof for spelling, formatting, and grammar. Have a consistent format and make sure it is perfect before sending it out. There is nothing worse than catching an error after you have already applied for several positions.

## 3.1. WHY CONSISTANT FORMATTING IS IMPORTANT

Consistent formatting is not only important for your resume, it will be important in your professional life as well. Keeping your documents neatly formatted and uniform shows a level of professionalism that few rarely master. I have seen so many resumes with multiple fonts, in various sizes throughout the document, that it made me question the level of education and experience of these individuals. If you can't take the time to neatly format a one to two-page resume, how can an employer trust you to care about your work? Resumes are often the first thing a potential employer will see of you. This is your chance to make a good first impression.

## 3.2. THE PROPER RESUME FORMAT

- **Text Font**: Times New Roman
- **Text Size**: 12pt Font
- Style each paragraph so that it is consistent throughout. Microsoft Word has incredible features to be able to accomplish this.
- Make sure your resume summary is relevant to the current position that you are applying to.

You are never going to have experience that translates 100% to any position that you apply for, but you need to make your resume show that to have applicable skills that fit the job. Applicant tracking systems are screening a database of thousands of resumes for keywords. If you don't have relevant experience, a recruiter will probably never know that you exist.

### 3.3. APPLICANT TRACKING SYSTEMS

Before going any deeper into the job searching process, you need to learn some valuable insights about applicant tracking systems (or "ATS"). ATS is used to filter through thousands of applications for a single position, to see who is the most qualified. While it does make a recruiter's job easier, it ensures that 99% of the time, a real human being will probably never read your resume or know that you exist. When writing a resume, you need to make sure your resume is robot friendly, to ensure that you have a chance of scoring an interview. Each resume needs to be tailored to each specific job that you apply for. You can say "goodbye" to the days of applying to as many places as possible with a single resume. This tactic does not increase your chances of getting an interview. In fact, this tactic basically ensures that your application will be rejected within 24 hours.

#### 3.3.1. HOW TO BEAT THE SYSTEM

Remember, a lot of recruiters are lazy (I'm sorry, I have to say it). There is absolutely no way they can read through every single resume to find someone who is perfectly qualified for the position.

Instead, recruiters and other job posters narrow the playing field, so that their work is more practical and less overwhelming (This happens in any industry). You really can't find anyone who is 100% a match for any position.

Your livelihood is on the line. This section is to help you beat the system, and score the interview, and get that job.

Your first objective in applying to a position is to scan for the following key words[1]:

| Keyword | Reason |
|---|---|
| Required | Don't fear the dreaded "R" word. Just try to find a way to professionally work what comes after it into your resume. If they require you to be a business professional and you lack the experience, find a way to say, "I am an aspiring business professional," somewhere in your resume. |
| Preferred | Don't let this this word or what comes after it scare you away. This simply means "would be nice." Even so, you need to find a way to add job related preferences to your resume. |

The above words are very important to look for because they show you exactly where the key words are. A recruiter/job poster will be looking for these key words in their ATS. Your job is to find a way to add these requirements and preferences to your resume. Remember, these additions must make sense and they need to show how they will bring value to the company. This matters to the company and the hiring manager; it should also matter to you. Don't simply add the skill to your resume. Show how you have used these skills to bring value to a previous position, or a project that you worked on, in any capacity.

Also, do not limit the length of your resume. ATS is a robot. Robots are not concerned with the length of your resume. It is only searching for key words. Don't be afraid to have a list section that lists all your relevant skills that apply to the job, based on the key words found on the job description.

# 4. HOW DO I LOOK FOR A BETTER JOB?

Looking for a new job is the easiest part of the process. You can rewrite your resume and apply to all kinds of positions all day if you would like. In fact, there are all kinds of resources available to you. In this chapter I am going to list some very good resources and then I am going to give you some helpful advice to avoid door-to-door marketing scams. You need a real job, with a consistent pay check. Never work for anyone who only pays you if you sell something. You might as well start your own business at that point, but that's a book for another day.

### 4.1. STARTING FROM SCRATCH

If you are new to the job market, or you haven't looked for a job in years. There are several approaches you can take. This first of which is, you will have to use technology. As I mentioned in chapter 3, most companies utilize an ATS. I have had many experiences trying to email an individual on the HR team, or even the hiring manager directly. In this modern age, the individuals in these companies do not really know how to react to you when you contact them outside of their sacred hiring process. I have had hiring managers and HR personnel ignore me, and even reject me for attempting to contact anyone directly to have a simple conversation, regardless of obvious qualifications. Not all of them have reacted this way, but you can expect this from the larger corporations. In the case of large companies, you may have to simply apply on the company's website and wait for a response. Large companies rely heavily on ATS to search through thousands of applications to easily find qualified candidates.

### 4.2. LINKEDIN

LinkedIn has made large strides to break the established norms of the current ATS drama. The website is like Facebook, but it is used for developing a professional network. Here, you will have access to job postings from various companies, in a wide variety of career fields. LinkedIn even provides you with the ability to directly message the job poster. However, many job postings do not give you access to the job poster.

Creating your profile on LinkedIn is like creating a resume. You will list your relevant skills, as well as your current and past positions. This is where you will tell the world how valuable you are as a worker. When creating a profile picture, you may want to have a professional business photo taken. You will find that many people have taken a similar approach. Your profile picture is often the first thing a potential employer sees when looking at your application on LinkedIn.

### 4.3. A WORD ABOUT JOB SCAMS

Job scams are jobs that claim to be one thing but are in fact something else. You will find that most job posting scams can be found on job posting sites. These scams are not regulated by the posting websites. For example, you will see a lot of jobs for the position of "Sales Executive." This job appears to be important because it has the word "executive" in the name. You apply to the position, and you get a phone call or email within 24-hours. The contacting individual asks if you would like to come in to discuss opportunities that are available with the company. Take note that you were not asked about the "Sales Executive" role that you applied for. This is the first red flag, the second is that your contact is not telling you what position that you would be interviewing for. At this point, you agree to meet to discuss a possible job opportunity. You are given an address with a date and time to meet with this person. The day of the interview, you go to meet this contact at the address that was given to you. When you get to the parking lot of the address, you see that it is a small shopping center parking lot, and none of the businesses carry the name of the company that you applied for. You call your contact to confirm the address and they inform you that it is accurate. They are waiting for you outside a grocery store in the shopping center, in a red car. You are curious to find out what's going on, and you meet the individual to get to the bottom of it. You find out that your contact is a low-level sales person, who sells cleaning supplies to businesses in the area. Your job will be to work under them, selling cleaning supplies to local businesses in the area as well.

If this story sounds too sounds too strange to be true, just be glad that its hasn't happened to you. Door-to-door scams like these take advantage of the unemployed and new college graduates who have never looked for a job before. If you know the signs, these scams are easy to avoid. Consider the following signs of a possible job scam:

- The contact will tell you that they would like to discuss **opportunities** but fails to tell you what job that you would be interviewing for. Companies with little to no information for you are hiding something. They know that no one wants to work for them.

- If you are not sure about a potential interview. Run a search online with the company's name, followed by the word "scam." This never fails. If a lot of other people have had issues with the company, they will take to the internet and let the whole world know. You should do the same and add to the public's knowledge of the scam. Do not allow yourself to be a victim of one of these scams.

- Research the position before applying. You can save yourself a lot of heartache by researching a position before applying.

These job scams may even contact you without even applying for a posted position. These contacts will still be similar. They will ask you if you are interested in discussing job opportunities with them. A legitimate recruiter will always tell you the position that will be discussed. You have no reason to speak to a recruiter if they have nothing to offer you. Don't ever do business with anyone who has nothing to bring to the table. You have much more power than you think you do.

# 5. I ACTUALLY GOT THE INTERVIEW... NOW WHAT?

Congratulations, you got the job interview for a legitimate job, with a legitimate company! I wish I could say that the job hunt is over, but this is where you determine if you really want the job. Don't have this idea that you must make the hiring manager or the HR team like you, because you have no control over that. This is where the hiring manager and the entire company shows how much they really want you as a candidate. To me, it should be immediately obvious if they want you for the job. Your resume should speak for itself. Don't jump through hoops for a company who won't do the same for you.

A job interview should be a simple conversation between two parties to determine if you want the job. There will be many occasions when you feel like you are a perfect fit for a role. You might get along with the hiring manager during the interview, but you are still rejected for the role, and you are never told why. You must understand that the hiring manager has personal attitudes that have been developed over a lifetime, and an ego that you could never possibly plan for. It could be possible that the hiring manager feels that you might outshine them. It would be best to try to not outshine the manager in the job interview, this will only go badly for you every single time. It's best to come off as experienced, but very interested in learning the new processes of the position. No matter who you are, you do not know everything, so do not come off as a know-it-all. In fact, prepare a list of relevant questions that are related to the position and the entire company. Relate these questions to research that you have already performed about the company and. Don't be afraid to ask the hiring manager to clarify anything about the position.

### 5.1. INTERVIEW PREPARATION

Typically, most job interviews start with a phone screening. A recruiter will either send you and email to schedule a phone screening, or they will attempt to call you and interview you on the spot. Never, under any circumstances, be a part of an interview that you are not prepared for. If you pick up the phone and they attempt to interview you then and there, inform them that this is not a good time for you, and request that they schedule a phone screening for another time. If they give you a hard time, let them know that you are no longer interested in the position. If they are that pushy before a phone screening, it's going to be worse if you get the job. Avoid all companies that have manipulative and unprofessional recruiters. They simply do not deserve you. Forget them faster than they forget you. Do not give them a second thought.

As soon as you have the phone screening scheduled, you will need to find the job description and start making notes on the key words that I told you about in chapter 3. These are going to be the points of the highest priority to the recruiter. They want to be able to provide a good candidate to the hiring manager, and it's your job to show how much of good fit you are for the position. You need to be able to show that you can provide great value to the company.

Research the hiring manager. A good recruiter and hiring manager will read your resume and conduct research on you. You should conduct your own research on the company and the hiring manager. Use LinkedIn to find out everything you can about the hiring manager. Your goal is to impress them and find common ground with them. Think of an interview with the hiring manager as a business negotiation. In any negotiation, both sides must bring something to the table. The hiring manager wants you to bring value to the company, and you want to be fairly compensated for your work. If an employer thinks they simply need to offer you employment at the bare minimum level of compensation, they are sorely mistaken. Have you ever heard the phrase "knowledge is power?" By doing your research, you can show up to an interview as a force to be reckoned with. You will be able to realize instantly if you are being taken advantage of. You will know if the employer really wants you as a candidate, or if they are simply trying to fill a job slot.

### 5.2. WHAT TO RESEARCH

- Your priority when an interview is on the table is to research a company's reputation. This method has saved me from so many fake job postings and door-to-door marketing scams. Use resources like Glassdoor Reviews[2] to see what is happening behind closed doors. Run a search online to see what people are saying about the company around the internet. How do the company's customers feel about it? All of this is important information. You can even post your own review on Glassdoor about the quality of your interview with the company. This is a good way to get a feel of the overall company culture.

- Is the company publicly traded? If the

company is publicly traded, you will have access to a company's financial information. This financial performance information is public knowledge for publicly traded companies, meaning everyone has access to it on the company's website. If the company is performing well, it may be a good bet that your employment will last for a while, if the company isn't performing well, you may want to inquire about how the position became vacant in the first place. You don't want to take a new job and get laid off within 90 days because the company needs to cut costs.

## 5.3. UNDERSTANDING THE MANAGER'S PERSPECTIVE

No one understands your perspective better than you. But when you finally get to meet the hiring manager, you need to think about their perspective. Their job is to determine if you are going to bring great value to the company or not. They want to know if you are going to enhance their team, and if you are going to make them look good as well. It would be a great idea to have a rehearsed statement prepared. You should be able to clearly define the great value that you would be able to bring to the position and the company.

# 6. WHAT TO DO WITH THIS WISDOM

Do not keep the information of this book to yourself. Now that you know the basics of how the job market operates, take what you have learned and share with others. It's plain as day that many companies could possibly improve their recruitment practices and application processes. Software companies could also need to provide companies with better tools that allow better communication to all job applicants, by telling them what skills they need to work on to improve their chances of being selected. The hiring process is too secretive and lacks the necessary feedback that many job seekers desperately need. Bottom line, the current system does not help the job seeker. These hiring processes are for the benefit of the hiring institutions alone. There is seldom affordable information available to those seeking employment, trying to make ends meet. In my opinion, this is simply unacceptable. My experience as a front-line employee has made me want to improve conditions for those individuals who feel like there are no alternatives to their low paying, exhausting jobs. These same individuals often feel that their voices are not being heard, and that there are absolutely no opportunities for advancement. Use the information in this book to educate people in your life, who feel like there is absolutely no way out of their situations. There is always a solution. You may have to work hard you get out of a terrible situation, but the work is well worth it.

I have seen so many people blame their companies for keeping them from promotion. My advice to them is find a company that will give you a promotion. No one can force you to stay with your company. If a company can neither respect you nor your talents, get out of there! This is the reason why websites such as Glassdoor exists, so the workers can finally hold their company's accountable for how they are being treated on the clock. Knowledge is power, so seek out a practical education, one that allows you to at least know your worth and when you are being taken advantage of. Companies can pay you whatever they want, but you don't have to work for them. Employment should always be a negotiation. If a competitor is willing to pay you more for the same amount of work, take the job, you are obviously worth it. The more skills you acquire, the higher your price tag. The same goes for years of experience, no matter if you are a cashier or the CEO of a fortune 500 company. If you want a better situation, go get it! The only person who can hold you back is you.

# 7.
# REFERENCES

Bureau of Labor Statistics. (2015, January 23). *Median weekly earnings by educational attainment in 2014*. Retrieved from Bureau of Labor Statistics: https://www.bls.gov/opub/ted/2015/median-weekly-earnings-by-education-gender-race-and-ethnicity-in-2014.htm

---

[1] If it makes you feel better, you can refer to these key words as "lazy words," these are the words that the typical recruiter or job poster is going to focus on the most.

[2] www.glassdoor.com